Tickle My Memory

by J. K. Schmauss
illustrated by Ethan Long

 HOUGHTON MIFFLIN   BOSTON

Copyright © by Houghton Mifflin Company. All rights reserved.

No part of this work may be reproduced or transmitted in any form or by any means, electronic or mechanical, including photocopying or recording, or by any information storage or retrieval system without the prior written permission of Houghton Mifflin Company unless such copying is expressly permitted by federal copyright law. Address inquiries to School Permissions, Houghton Mifflin Company, 222 Berkeley Street, Boston, MA 02116.

Printed in China

ISBN 10: 0-618-89988-X
ISBN 13: 978-0-618-89988-3

15 16 17 18 0940 21 20 19 18

4500695557

Fives

Josh: What's five Q times two Q?
Leo: Ten Q.
Josh: You're welcome!

5, 10, 15, 20 . . .
Count by fives and
you'll have plenty.

Take the number 35.
Divide by 7—you'll get 5.

Sixes

I had a friend named Kevin,
His age was 6 × 7.
On his cake were 42
Candles that he blew and blew.

Hungry chicks 6 × 6
Eat one worm each,
That's 36.

How many groups of 6 in 54?
9 groups only, no less, no more.

Sevens

Some animals came in today—
I counted 7 × 4.
Better open up the door—
Here come 28 more!

Roses are red,
Violets are blue,
7 × 6 is 42.

Seven packs of gum I have,
Each has 8 big sticks.
If I open up my mouth real wide,
I can chew all 56!

Say this little poem with me.
7 × 9 is 63.
When 63 is divided by 9,
The answer is 7 all the time.

7 × 7 is 49.
You are so cool,
You are so fine!

Eights

Dora: When do chickens have 8 feet?
Wapi: When there are 4 of them.

Try to catch Flight 6 × 8!
It's leaving from Gate 48.

Groups of 8 in 24
Isn't tricky anymore
Since I talked to my friend Lee
And he told me that it's 3.

My dog Jake knows lots of tricks,
Like 8 × 7 is 56.
He'd like to do one just for you—
8 × 9 is 72!

Read·Think·Write 6 × 8 = 48. How can you use division to show a math fact from the same fact family?

Nines

To remember multiplication facts for 9, use your hands: Hold them out, fingers spread wide. Want to know how much 9×4 is? Start at the left and bend down your fourth finger. There should be three fingers to the left of your bent finger. Write a 3. There should be six fingers to the right of your bent finger. Write a 6 after the 3. The answer is 36. Go ahead and try it out. It works!

To multiply a number by 9, multiply it first by 10 and then subtract the number from the product.

Elevens

To multiply 11 by a two-digit number, add the two digits and then put the sum between them.

25 × 11 = 275
31 × 11 = 341
57 × 11 = 627 (You'll need to carry the 1!)

See if you can figure out how multiplying 11 by a three-digit number works.

253 × 11 = 2,783
117 × 11 = 1,287
532 × 11 = 5,852
267 × 11 = 2,937

(Hint: Look at the first problem. Write the first number. Add the first and second digits. Add the second and third digits. Write the last number.)

Read·Think·Write What is 43 × 11? What is 361 × 11?

Twelves

Sally: Why doesn't your math class have desks?

Mark: Because we use times tables.

Carmen: Where can you buy a ruler that is 3 feet long?

Alberto: At a yard sale.

Into the depths did the diver delve,
Down 7 feet multiplied by 12.
"Great!" she cried as she hit 84
And found she'd reached the ocean floor!

In the library I did shelve
A total of books that was 9×12.
I lined them up and made them straight,
Every last book—all 108.

What's 72 divided by 12?
It is exactly 6.
It's the same as 6×12.
That's one of math's cool tricks.

Responding — Vocabulary

1. Which of the following does not belong in the fact family for 8?
   A. 8 × 6
   B. 11 × 8
   C. 9 × 6

2. **Solve Problems/Make Decisions** What is the product of the following expressions?
   A. 8 × 3
   B. 6 × 4

3. What are two factors of 56?

Activity

- Make bingo cards showing products for fact families 7–12. Make each card different.
- Have one player from your group call out a multiplication or division fact (for example, 8 × 6), while the others look for the answer on their bingo cards.
- When you have found all the answers in a row (up, down, or sideways), call out "Bingo!"